INSIDE THE WAVE

Helen Dunmore (1952-2017) was a poet, novelist, short story and children's writer. Her poetry books received a Poetry Book Society Choice and Recommendations, the Alice Hunt Bartlett Award, and the Signal Poetry Award. *Bestiary* was shortlisted for the T.S. Eliot Prize in 1997, and *Inside the Wave* is shortlisted for the 2017 Costa Poetry Award. She won first prize in the Cardiff International Poetry Competition in 1990 with her poem 'Sisters leaving the dance', and first prize in the National Poetry Competition in 2010 with 'The Malarkey'.

After making her debut with *The Apple Fall* in 1983, Helen Dunmore published all her poetry with Bloodaxe Books. Her earlier work is available in *Out of the Blue: Poems 1975-2001* (2001), which was followed by *Glad of These Times* (2007), *The Malarkey* (2012), and *Inside the Wave* (2017), her tenth and final collection.

She published twelve novels and three books of short stories with Penguin, including *A Spell of Winter* (1995), winner of the Orange Prize for Fiction, *Talking to the Dead* (1996), *The Siege* (2001), *Mourning Ruby* (2003), *House of Orphans* (2006) and *The Betrayal* (2010), as well as *The Greatcoat* (2012) with Hammer, and *The Lie* (2014) *Exposure* (2016) and *Birdcage Walk* (2017) with Hutchinson.

Born in Beverley, Yorkshire, she studied English at York University, and after graduating in 1973 spent two years teaching in Finland before settling in Bristol.

HELEN DUNMORE

Inside the Wave

BLOODAXE BOOKS

ISBN: 978 1 78037 358 4

First published 2017 by
Bloodaxe Books Ltd,
Eastburn,
South Park,
Hexham,
Northumberland NE46 1BS.

Second impression June 2017
(with additional poem on page 69).
Third impression December 2017.

www.bloodaxebooks.com
For further information about Bloodaxe titles
please visit our website or write to
the above address for a catalogue.

Supported using public funding by
ARTS COUNCIL
ENGLAND

Cover design: Neil Astley & Pamela Robertson-Pearce.

Printed in Great Britain by Bell & Bain Limited, Glasgow, Scotland, on
acid-free paper sourced from mills with FSC chain of custody certification.

for Susan Glickman

ACKNOWLEDGEMENTS

Acknowledgements are due to the editors of the following publications and websites where some of these poems first appeared: *Acumen, The Guardian, Hwaet! 20 Years of Ledbury Poetry Festival*, ed. Mark Fisher (Bloodaxe Books/Ledbury Poetry Festival, 2016), *London Magazine, 1914: Poetry Remembers*, ed. Carol Ann Duffy (Faber & Faber, 2014), *100 Prized Poems: twenty-five years of the Forward Books*, ed. William Sieghart (Faber & Faber, 2016), and *The Poetry Review*.

Several of the poems were broadcast on *The Verb* (BBC Radio 3).

The poem 'Hold out your arms' on page 69 was added to the second impression of this book.

CONTENTS

Counting Backwards

Untroubled, the anaesthetist
Potters with his cannula
As the waterfall in the ante-room
Grows steadily louder,

All of them are cool with it
And just keep on working
No wonder they wear Wellingtons –
I want to ask them

But it seems stupid, naive,
Even attention-seeking.
Basalt, I think, the rock
Where the white stream leaps.

Imagine living at such volume
Next door to a waterfall,
Stepping in and out of the noise
In their funny clothes.

But you can get used to anything
Like the anaesthetist
Counting to himself
Backwards, all wrong.

The Underworld

And besides, we might play cards:
Those slapdash games you once taught me
Which any fool can remember
Or from the fabric which has been tied
With string, wrapped in brown paper
Put away in the highest cupboard
Since the time the children were young
And everyone's children were young
I might make new curtains
And hem them all by hand.

I used to be so afraid of failing
To grasp the moment, the undertone,
To look foolish in the eyes of anyone
But now I like the patter of cards
The lazy sandwich that falls open
Halfway to the mouth,
The refills in a thumbed glass
The way people get up, yawn,
Go stiff-legged to the window, wondering
That it isn't yet tomorrow

It's a long way from here to the river:
I like to see the fish come in
But the game is still on.
From the way the cards are falling
I'd say you will win.
I used to think it was a narrow road
From here to the underworld
But it's as broad as the sun.
I say to you: I have more acquaintance
Among the dead than the living
And I am not pretending.
It's pure fact, like this sandwich
Which hasn't quite tempted anyone.

Shutting the Gate

A barefoot girl hugs the wall
On tiptoe, her instep
Arched like a cat's back.
Nearby a car revs.
She looks at me and smiles
Like a primary-school child.
Her friend smokes by the gate
One hand on the wall.
Lissom as lilies, they shake dark curls
And watch the car.

I say: Are you girls all right?
And she says: We don't like
The look of them. Two men
In the dark of the car, also smoking.
She swings the gate shut.
They might be my daughters –
A little older, I reckon –
But those men don't look
Much like the sons of anyone.

It's late, almost two a.m.
They are both inside the gate
With one shoe-strap broken
A packet of cigarettes
Brief lovely dresses.
I ask: Will you be all right?
They don't want to come inside,
They just didn't like the gate open
When those men were waiting
Like that, with the engine going
And from time to time a rev
So we don't forget.

In Praise of the Piano

In praise of the piano that slips out of tune
I raise my needle from the dusty record
And watch the vinyl turn and turn,

In praise of the unrepeatable, the original,
The one thought clinging to the one word
I dip my nib into the inkwell,

In praise of the only known photograph
Of your great-grandmother, I hoard
Film, blackout, developing bath.

O needle jumping on dusty vinyl
O letter stuffed in dirty pigeonhole
The fragile, the original
The one word before the blot falls.

Finger ballet on the telephone switchboard,
The one word that flows from the lips
And the one heart by which it is heard

Unrepeatable, fragile. In praise
Of all that cleaves to the note, then slips
From it, and never stays.

Re-opening the old mines

But you would have to go below
The bare bright surface. And I suppose
Out of the dark would come marching
Men with tattoos
Of dust on their forearms,
And as for the gorse burning its own fuse
Or the boy who drops to his knees

Shuffling along his seam
Towards the pock of an explosion
Heard from above, miles out
In the fishing grounds,
He's in the shop, serving
Eighty flavours of ice cream.
Drip drip goes brown water
Into the shaft while harebells quiver.

Under the houses there's a cavern
So deep that when the camera
Was lowered it swung pendulum
While the void kept opening
But I suppose that in the veiny dark
Tunnels that knit the rock
They are still blasting,
And ponies which never see the light
Snuff sugar and are content

As may be among the rare metals:
Antimony, molybdenum,
Wolframite, uranium
Gold, silver and indium.

Inside the Wave

And when at last the voyage was over
The ship docked and the men paid off,
The crew became a scattering
Dotted, unremarkable,
In houses along the hill top
Where the lamps flared in welcome
And then grew dim, where a woman turned
As if from habit to the wall.

In the bronze mirror there was a woman
Combing what was left of her hair
And beside her, grimacing,
A dirty old mariner.
He swore and knocked back the chair.

Yes, then Odysseus opened his mouth
And all that was left
Was the sound an old man makes
Between a laugh and a cough.
His toenails were goat's hooves
His hair a wild
Nest of old stories,

He straddled the tiles
As a man of the sea does
But she would not touch
His barnacled lips.
From the fountain, pulse by pulse
Came gouts of blood.

Everything stayed as it was,
There was no unravelling
Of wake behind him,
No abandoning
Unwanted memories and men.
Besides, the earth stank.

He went down to the black rock
Where the sea pours
And the white sand blows,
He turned his back to the land
And thought of nothing
For the voyage was over,
The ship dragged by a chain
Onto the ramp for inspection.

The waves turned and turned
Neither toward nor away from him,
Swash and backwash
Crossing, repeating,
But never the same.
At the lip of the wave, foam
Stuttered and broke,

It was on the inside
Of the wave he chose
To meditate endlessly
Without words or song,
And so he lay down
To watch it at eye-level,
About to topple
About to be whole.

Odysseus to Elpenor

But tell me, Elpenor
Now that I have conjured you
From those caverns so deep
No camera can fathom them

Now you have come to drink the wine
Poured on the ground in libation
And slake your fleshless appetite
On the snuff of blood,

Tell me how you came here
Fleeing like a cloud shadow
Over restless water –
You frighten me, Elpenor.

Look, I have drawn my sword
Are you not afraid?
You were a handsome fighter –
Will you come on?

Take the heat of my hand
Elpenor, between your palms.
Bow your head for a blessing
Houseless boy, and now tell me

How you came to die.
We are not heroes, any of us,
Only familiars
Of grey shores and the sea-pulse,

Laggards, like the tide.
Was it you, Elpenor
Who rowed when the wind died
Until your hands bled?

You fell asleep in Circe's house
Drunk, like all of us,
Playing the fool
As you plunged from the roof.

When your neck broke
We were already racing
Down to the harbour
Where our black ship quivered,

Even when our sails filled
And we scudded before the wind
We could not catch your shadow.
We had left you behind

But you are ahead of us
Waiting, unpropitiated
Poor boy, unburied
Come to lap at the blood.

Dawn pushes away night's curtain
Your body must be burned
And your hair tied with ribbons
As a remembrance.

You ask me in the name of my son
Not to let you be forgotten
But to build your grave mound
Where the pebbles meet the tide

'And thrust into its heart my oar
So that I may row myself forever.'

Plane tree outside Ward 78

The tree outside the window
Is lost and gone,
Billow of leaf in the summer dark,
A buffet of rain.

I might owe this tree to morphine,
I might wake in the morning
To find it dissolved, paper
Hung in water,

Nothing to do with dreams.
I cannot sleep.
Pain is yards away
Held off like bad weather,

In the ward's beautiful contentment
Freed by opiates.
Hooked to oxygen
We live for the moment.

The shaft

I don't need to go to the sun –
It lies on my pillow.

Without movement or speech
Day deepens its sweetness.

Sea shanties from the water,
A brush of traffic,

But it's quiet here.
Who would have thought that pain

And weakness had such gifts
Hidden in their rough hearts?

Leave the door open

Leave the door open! We cheep and command
From the shared double bed or from the cot
With bars that make tigers out of the dark.
We want the fume and coil of your cigarettes,
The smoke that has embraced us from birth,

The click of your footsteps on the wooden landing,
The wedge of light that parts us from the dark
As I hold, hold to it like a sword.
Leave the door open. Go downstairs, go out
After priming the neighbours to listen,

Go to your world: the cider-bottle cap
Askew on its stem, the pellucid gin,
The ashtray overflowing with stubs,
Radio laughter and suppressed voices
As you creak upstairs without waking us,

But don't forget to leave the light on
So the spill of it falls where it must.
We can breathe now in our coffin of sheets
So tangled we can't get out of them,
As long as you leave the door open.

My life's stem was cut

My life's stem was cut,
But quickly, lovingly
I was lifted up,
I heard the rush of the tap
And I was set in water
In the blue vase, beautiful
In lip and curve,
And here I am
Opening one petal
As the tea cools.
I wait while the sun moves
And the bees finish their dancing,
I know I am dying
But why not keep flowering
As long as I can
From my cut stem?

The Bare Leg

There we sat in the clattering dark
As the carriages swayed downhill
Under London's invisible rivers,
There our faces were mute
With a day of burdens
As we recovered ourselves,

Some read star signs from a column
In a left-behind newspaper,
Some sighed and shut their eyes.
When the train came to a halt
For nothing in the dark of the tunnel
We breathed out silence

And when the voice came
Lulling with news of a red signal
We sighed again and rolled our eyes
Or adjusted our standing positions
To lean into one another more gently

And if we had room to turn our heads
We looked down the long corridor
Of carriages aligned
As if the driver had drawn them
Onto the straight, and left them perfect

And in the next-to-one carriage
Less crowded than our own
A bare leg stretched into the aisle
Taking up room
As if this were a beach in summer.

We studied the delicate anatomy
Of shin and knee

The putting together and planting
Of toe and heel
The tension of thigh,

And beyond it nothing
For the body was hidden
By the bulk of a boy
Inopportunely leaning
To adjust his headphones.

As if this were a beach in summer
The leg took its own time
And flexed luxuriously
While the signal held against us
And delay surged into time

Lost, irrecoverable.
The driver told us again
We would be on the move shortly
But no one believed him.
This was what we had always known

Was about to happen: the calf tightening
The vessel of the hip cupping
The thrust of the bare leg,
The naked precision of the human
As it steps into action,

And down the long corridor, swaying
As the train resumed,
The chant, the murmur
Of foot soles, someone
Merely walking into the next room.

The Place of Ordinary Souls

In such meadows the days pass
Without shadow, unremarkable.
On time, the bus pants at its halt,
Passengers peel their thighs
From hot vinyl, and step down.

Swift-heeled Achilles strides
Through the fields of asphodel
Flanked by heroes and warriors
Who have left their mark on the earth
And want nothing to do with us.

With impatient glance at the starry fields
And kit on their backs, they're gone
Route-marching to Elysium
Where the gods are at home.
We are glad to see the back of them.

In the fields of asphodel we dawdle
Towards the rumour of a beauty spot
Which turns out to be shut.
No matter. Why not get out the picnic
And see if the tea's still hot?

The bus shuttles all day long
With its cargo of ordinary souls.
We lie on our backs, eyes closed,
Dreaming of nothing while clouds pass.

(According to Greek legend, ordinary, unheroic souls pass the afterlife
in the fields of asphodel.)

My daughter as Penelope

Seven years old last birthday,
With waist-length hair,
White tunic, yellow ribbon
Threaded at neck and hem,

She has learned her lines,
The chalked-in positions,
The music which means
She must come out of the wings.

In the dusty cave of the theatre
The children's bare feet patter.
My daughter thrusts out her arm
And beats her suitors,

In pride at the laughter
She forgets the pause,
But chides them, berates them
Like an abandoned woman

Who has over cold years learned
To preserve the hearth.
Odysseus, so long expected
Would scarcely be welcome –

A man of many distractions
At this very moment
Oblivious of her
Conjuring the dead with blood.

My daughter as Penelope
Shakes back her hair and cries
That they should all go home
Here they will get nothing,

While the little capering boys
Evade her blows.

I made her tunic, I threaded
Those ribbons at neck and hem,
I brushed and loosened her hair.
She leaned against my shoulder

In pure naïvety. 'I didn't know
You could make anything
As good as this,' she said.
The theatre swallowed the child.

We thought they were too young for it,
They would freeze, or be afraid,
But they were blithe, barefoot,
Running from the underworld

To butt like kids against the white sheet
That marked the kingdom of the dead.
The skin rose on our arms
The hairs prickled. They'd gone.

My daughter as Penelope
Seven years old, thrusting
Her bare arm out of her chiton
Pushing away her suitors

As one may do in childhood.
The sheet quivered
For the dead could barely contain
Their desire for the living

And the play was long.
The cave of the stage grew vast —
A mouth without a tongue
Consuming our children.

The Lamplighter

Here, where the old Industrial School was
And then the porn-film sheds,
Stands the last lamp before the water.
Dead as he's been these ninety years
The lamplighter on his beat
Walks with ladder on shoulder.
Above the Mardyke Steps and the donkey track
He fixes ladder to pole, stands back
Then climbs nimbly into the mass of flower.
His head is a ball of petals. He barely coughs
As the soft skin of petunia
Plasters itself against his nostrils.

Now he takes up his torch
Tips the lever and touches the gas.
A big rude flower, a dahlia
Blooms in its case.
There are boys slouched against the wall
Up to no good, there are white-faced girls
Running to the shop for a paper of chips.
There's the long fall of the Mardyke Steps
Tunneling the bad way to the docks
And so the lamplighters muster
To stop the thieves who can knock you down
Between one lamp and the next,
Between one step and the drop.

The Halt

We stop somewhere on the plain
While I am sleeping. As my book slips
The man opposite leans to stop it
Still chomping that sausage he cut
With a penknife opened and cleaned
On his sleeve, long before I slept.

He pulls down the window-strap and at once
We hear birds scurry in the scrub
That bows and knits to the cuff of the wind.
I turn my face to the glass
For I speak his language painfully
Sentence by sentence, and he will talk to me.

We have halted for no reason
In the white glare of noon
At this shack surrounded by sunflowers
Pothering hens and a plot of maize
Beyond which the land gallops unbroken.
There is also a woman

Who swings a bucket on her arm
As she clambers the makeshift platform
Box upon box, skilfully placed.
She knows all the long curve of the train.
Now from the engine a stoker swings
A stream of water that dings on the iron.

The rails flash so I can barely look at them.
Our engine shucks steam as it canters
Panting, pulling against the brake.
The bucket clangs. The woman steps down.
From my sticky mouth the words come:
Hens, maize, sunflowers,
Her bowed head and the way she waits.

Bluebell Hollows

Are they blue or not blue?
All I know is the smoke
That moves under the trees,

In Tremenheere Woods
Moths clung to the sheet,
It was the hour of innocence –

We developed flowers
On light-sensitive paper:
They are still here.

We could never walk fast enough,
Seven year olds
Up in the dead of night

Climbing to the lookout
Where bonfires blazed
For reasons long forgotten,

But perhaps because the Romans
Once came this far
To walk the bluebell hollows.

A Loose Curl

I have never known you easily
Hold my hand as you do now.
We sit here for hours.

There's salt all over the glass
And however I look to the horizon
Not a sail to be seen.

I hold your hand and say nothing.
Once I must have held
Your finger, a loose curl.

You remember in snatches.
You say you're afraid of a whale
Snorkelling through the blue Arctic.

The ice is so fragile.
You must spread your weight, like this
And inch out to the abyss.

This is not a glacier, it's only
A world of ice falling apart.
I think something is moving slowly

Deep in your fingers.
The sea stays in its lair
But wants to be where we are.

Hornsea, 1952

...I by the tide
Of Humber would complain...

Yes, but were we happy then?
The wind blew from the east, you were always cold,
And there was a boating lake –
Water trapped on your left, below sea level,
Murkily waiting to be stirred by boys with sticks.

You and I must have been conspirators
All those cold days. The two of us.
No books, no essays, no bike propped up
In happy rush. No clangour of bells
Or notes in pigeon-holes:
I can't wait for you, my darling.

Huge planes take off
Overhead into loneliness,
You bake sponge cakes at four o'clock
For belated homecomings –
Men drink in the Mess.

The fortune-teller saw you kneel
Beside your trunk, packing, unpacking.
The hour for scholarship came round again:
You won. You win
And write Oxford on labels
Flowingly, beneath your name.

A small child drags at your hand.
Another pushes out your belly-button.
You haul at the pram.
The two of us. How the wind blows.
You lose one child and you keep one.
You will change your accent for no one.

You could write an essay on this:
A sozzled officer slow to come home,
Marvell's vegetable kingdom,
World enough and time,
Another baby fattening
And your thirtieth birthday on the horizon.

Festival of stone

(for Jitka Palmer)

The chink of hammers is a song
Like blackbirds interrupted, alarming
One another in the beauty of the morning

Over the thud of mallets, raspings on stone
As the sculptors bend and sweat
And the skirts of the tents blow out.

The chink of hammers is the wind that plays
On plane leaves keyed to a ripple
In the updraught from the water

And all is flash and shatter
As the surface breaks open
To show the face of the stone.

A Bit of Love

He must stir himself. No more hiding
Behind the skill of hands
That are not his.

Those nurses are good girls.
They'll do anything for you –
Within reason of course.

He must fumble his old fingers
Get himself moving –
They all say this.

Ambulance bells carouse
Until he doesn't know where he is.
Drunks in the street

Swaying about like Holy Moses
That's about the size of it:
No one listens.

The lamplighter went home years ago
There's no night policeman
Or dawn milk-chink.

That stout world is a trinket
In the eyes of his grandchildren.
His shifts are over.

Here's a bit of paper
And a book to lean on
What more does he want?

In his well-taught hand-writing
He'll send her a bit of love
To make her blush.

Winter Balcony with Dunnocks

Close to the earth, creeping, lowly
Mouse-coloured, unglamorous
Dunnocks, your dusty wings flirt
In the dry roots of ivy, you are unnoted
Untweeted creatures, you turn
Dry leaves and peck for grubs.

You come to my balcony, a cloud of you
Eight floors up and slender-dark
Tilting your wings to skirt the railing
And flicker among the geraniums
As the winter cold comes on –
Quick, quick, against the dusk.

You don't care that someone was here
Before you: those two fat pigeons
Dumpily purring, the noisy ones
Who think I can't see where they slump
Between flower-pot and plastic bucket
Breast to breast, at roost –

No, you are too quick-dark
On the rim of night, flickering
Through the chill buds of the camellia,
Unnoted, untweeted creatures,
Dunnocks, foraging
December and the year's husk.

Mimosa

Why is the mimosa here
Inside its dark frame?

So down-to-earth, it comes out workmanlike
Year after year, breaks its own branches
With plumes that make the sky quiver.

Let's sit here, on the bench, under it
To rest while you get your breath.

Winter's over, and look, in this dustbin
Someone has planted wallflowers.
There's pollen all over your arms.

Nightfall in the IKEA Kitchen

Nightfall in the IKEA kitchen.
Even though the lights are left on
I feel the push of the wind's deconstruction
Take the hull of the shed by storm.

Creak and strain of test and fault-finding
But here in the glow I am alone
Expected and consoled. Here is the notice board
Riddled with reminders and invitations,

Here are picture ledges and high cabinets
Kitchen trolley, drying racks
A sly shoe cabinet, fabric pocket-ties:
A life so sweetly cupboarded

I barely believe it is mine. Open
And another light comes on
Here is the place where I begin again
As a twenty-three year old Finn

Taking the keys of her first home.
I use space well here. I waste nothing.
The floor clock has shelves, the bed lifts up
And if I yield and sleep

I will become part of the storage system
Harbouring dreams and heat.
Everything is a little below scale
And therefore ample. Stuva, Dröma

Expedit, Tromsø, Isfjorden...
I rock in the peace of their names
Even as I mispronounce them
For this is nightfall in the one-bedroom

Model apartment's kitchen
When everyone has gone home
And there is nothing left
But the Marketplace itself.

And say a child is born, no problem.
With a simple room-divider
I can create not only child storage
But also a home office

From which I will provide for us both.
Look, here is his football on the floor
And here a shelf where it may be stored.
His whole life is in these drawers.

Call him Billy and see him run.
When he grows up and moves out
Just take down the partition
To have, at last, my own space again.

Ten thousand times the wind has pushed the doors
But they have not opened yet.
Those cupboards. Stockholm. Yes, that green
Nature can never quite get.

The Duration

Here they are on the beach where the boy played
For fifteen summers, before he grew too old
For French cricket, shrimping and rock pools.

Here is the place where he built his dam
Year after year. See, the stream still comes down
Just as it did, and spreads itself on the sand

Into a dozen channels. How he enlisted them:
Those splendid spades, those sun-bonneted girls
Furiously shoring up the ramparts.

Here they are on the beach, just as they were
Those fifteen summers. She has a rough towel
Ready for him. The boy was always last out of the water.

She would rub him down hard, chafe him like a foal
Up on its legs for an hour and trembling, all angles.
She would dry carefully between his toes.

Here they are on the beach, the two of them
Sitting on the same square of mackintosh,
The same tartan rug. Quality lasts.

There are children in the water, and mothers patrolling
The sea's edge, calling them back
From the danger zone beyond the breakers.

How her heart would stab when he went too far out.
Once she flustered into the water, shouting
Until he swam back. He was ashamed of her then.

Wouldn't speak, wouldn't look at her even.
Her skirt was sopped. She had to wring out the hem.
She wonders if Father remembers.

Later, when they've had their sandwiches
She might speak of it. There are hours yet.
Thousands, by her reckoning.

At the Spit

If you lie down at the Spit on this warm
But sunless afternoon, here on the pebbles,
Smelling the wrack and sea-blown plastic,
If you squint at the clouds that sag on the horizon
Without bringing rain or allowing the sun,
If you lie down here in the hollow
And take your backpack for a pillow
And watch how the pebbles lose colour
And then, shutting your eyes, listen,
You'll hear the tide swell and the wrack dry
To fool's balloons, incurably saline
Crackling under the weight of your backpack
As you lie down,

If you lie down and as they say do nothing
You'll hear the tongue of the tide licking
The Spit – O fine appetite! – You'll hear the click
And tumble of pebbles, slumbrous
Geography shifting: this is the land mass
And this the plastic, the wrack, the mess
To pick over in search of a home. Go back,
It's late and the unseen sun's dropping
Hurts the clouds and turns them to rain.
Drowsy, at home, you lie and dream
Of longboats and long-shed blood
Of corner shops and running for sweets –
O sweet familiarity, geography
Melting into the known –

Terra Incognita

And now we come to the unknown land
With its blue coves and inlets where sweet water
Bubbles against the salt. Its sand
Is ready for footprints. Give me your hand

Onto the rock where the seaweed clings
And the red anemone throbs in its crevice
Through swash and backwash. These things
Various as the brain's comb and the tide's swing

Or the first touch of untouched terrain
On our footsoles, as the land explores us,
Have become our fortune. Let me explain
Which foods are good to eat, and which poison.

Four cormorants, one swan

The swans go up with slow wing-beats
That strike off from the surface of the water.
Even the most absorbed games-player
Deep in his mobile, looks up at the clatter
Of six swans' wings.

After the swans have patrolled their harbour
They settle singly. One drifts with the current
To the house-boat window that always opens,
Another sails towards two cormorants
Hanging out their wings

And two coosing, or fishing
In the shallows beside the jetty.
Now the whole afternoon hangs
In the balance between four cormorants
And a single swan, approaching.

The first cormorant pratfalls from its perch
In an ungainly bundle of wings
Or so it seems. But no, it is flying
Arrowlike to a fish a hundred yards off.
A lover could not be more direct.

Girl in the Blue Pool

Years back and full of echoes.
Chlorine, urine, raucous
Cuff of voices on broken surface.
A boy on the edge rowdily teeters
And you, knees flexed, arms back
Are on the pulse of your stroke. Suppose
It is you, now, in the pink bikini, close
To making five hundred metres
As the ceiling splinters with echoes.

Suppose you touch the tiles on the turn
And vanish. The churn
Of bubbles streams at your heels
While you shake water out of your ears
To catch the voice of your instructor
Who paces you, outpaces you
On the blue-wet tiles. How her voice echoes.
You should not be wearing a bikini
And you were slow on the turn.

I am years back and full of echoes.
The silver stream where you swim
Has long ago been swallowed,
But at your temples the lovely hollows
Play in June light. Suppose
There is one length left in you, knees flexed
Arms back. Chlorine, urine, raucous
Voices on shattered surface. If that boy topples
You too will go down.

February 12th 1994

No one else remembers that room
With the blood pressure cuff and the plastic cot
And the bag on its stand dripping
Millilitre by millilitre
When the visitors had gone home
And the tyres six storeys down
Skidded, infrequent.

Snow on the window ticked
The glass, becoming sleet
And the sheets for all their stains were white.
No one else remembers that room
Where you cried each time the lights
Went off and the nurses were absent
For hours by morphia time,

I reached for you in pain
And lifted you in your hospital nightgown
To wedge you against me
For we were both falling
You with purple, dangling limbs
Ecstatic, all lips
And quick, hot breathing,

I watching a nurse who did not exist
Write her hieroglyphics
As the snow thickened.
I made a vow to you then
In our solitude
That you would never remember,
With two fingers I smoothed the ruck
Of the gown against your back.

What shall I do for my sister in the day she shall be spoken for?

I have a little sister, she has no breasts.
I buy her face covering at the shop
Where they have nearly run out.
So, we are lucky. Black cloth sucks
Into her nostrils. My sister screams.

When she's finished saying she can't breathe
When I've cleaned the snot from her face
And rearranged her so she'll be safe
I say: It's for your own good.
Do as I do and walk close.

I have a little sister, she has no breasts.
She would like to be an ophthalmologist.
When she was three she had a cyst
Removed from under her left eyelid.
I say: Don't cry, you can still see out.

I tell her to walk between me and the wall
And keep her eyes downward. We scuttle
Like crabs in a black wrapping.
We shall buy rice, we shall go home.
What shall I do for my sister
In the day when she shall be spoken for?

In Secret

And this is where they met in secret.
Follow my pointing finger. Now you see it
Quite empty. Those curtains that veiled it

Are rags, and the bed stripped bare.
Here she played for him, there
He placed his shoes in the corner.

Piano from an upstairs room,
Wanton extravagance of scales falling
As we imagine birdsong –

But only slow it down
And hear the gong-repeat of a rhythm
Like the treading of rubble over a woman.

All the breaths of your life

There is a gargoyle look when the mouth caves.
No more words can be hoped for, the lips
Are not for speaking, the tongue
Is all sag and distortion.

I might think that your kindness is effaced.
No more look can be hoped for, your eyes
Are not for seeing, the skin
Is a drawn curtain over them.

I hear your breath, now failing
As all the breaths of your life become
Petals endlessly opening
Inward, where the dark is.

Her children look for her

Life and death are in the hands of God she said
As a boat is in the hands of the dark water,

And now her children look for her
In the zizz of her sewing-machine each evening
And the smell of cardamom.

She said: life and death are in the hands of God.
As the sun beat on the roof of the van
She closed her eyes to dream,

And her children look as the Pole Star goes up
Close to the moon.

Little papoose

If I were the moon
With a star papoose
In the windy sky
I'd carry my one star home,

If I were the sea
With boats in my arms
On this cold morning
I'd carry them,

If I were sleeping
And my dream turned
I would carry you
Little papoose
Wherever you choose.

Cliffs of Fall

(to the memory of Gerard Manley Hopkins)

Spring of turf and thrift, tangle of fleece, sheep-shit,
Subtle flowers where honeybees knock
At the foxglove lip and the gorse trap

Then sheer on our left the drop. Spatter of bracken hooks
Misleading the lambs. In the bank, marsh violets
Wet, lovely, minute. We need not look for the fall, the chink

Of pebble that tumbles. All the grey scree stirs
Slip-rattles and stills itself. Here is the slope's
Angle, implacable. Here's where you look

Touch, unbalance, dislodge. Infinite drop
Where the bee burrs at the foxglove's lip,
All quick-tongued, intimate.

Time to step back to the wide margin
Cleave to the path's dapper attention
Unspring each poem,

Pitch each new note to the key of loss,
Lose nothing. Stay clear of the drop
Where the world bursts through its dirty glass.

Sun on your neck, a dazzle of violets
Infinitely slipsliding –
No quick wing-beat of flight, but a slope

Of gravel-rubble, its angle implacable
stripping you raw. From here your fall
Is a matter of form: a slow marvel.

Five Versions from Catullus

1 *Through Babel of Nations*

Through babel of nations and waste of water
I come my brother. What are these rites to us?
Your ashes are speechless
My words falter.

Blind fate has taken you, brother,
You and I are undone.
The wine I bring you is spoiled
With the salt of parting –
What else can I give?
Only a last greeting.

2 *Undone*

What you have done to me has undone me.
You have led me so far from myself
That my mind loses its bearings.
Even if you shape-shifted
To your best and dearest
I couldn't care for it. Dark love drives me on.

3 *Sirmio*

Almost island and jewel of all islands
In lakes stiller than thought or in wild oceans
Sweet or salt as the sea-god makes them,
Sirmio,

I see you, all of you, I take you in
I see you, barely believing
I've left those featureless, endless Bithynian plains.

We travel over many waters
To reach home-coming,
Struggle and suffering over, the mind dissolved
Of all its troubles, burdens laid down –
The soft bed waits for our exhaustion.

I see you, all of you, I know your
Confusion of ripples against the lakeshore
Welcoming laughter
The sounds of home
Ringing like masts in harbour:
Sirmio.

4 Dedication

My slim volume, polished almost to nothing –
Shall I dedicate it to you, Cornelius?

You thought something of my songs
Even though you were the only man in Italy

Who could wrap up the world in three tomes
Of flawless erudition.

My God, your learning and labour
Lean heavily against my little volume,

So take my book, this fingernail's width
For what it's worth.

5 *Sparrow*

Sparrow, my girl's delight
And plaything held to her breast,
Sparrow whom she teases with one finger
Daring your littleness to peck harder –
Sparrow, I burn for her
And crave the smallest crumb
As the pair of you play
Folded together in rapture
Under one wing.
I too long to comfort her
In grief or oppressive longing –
If only I could play with her as you do
Until she forgets her soul's sadness.

Rim

Here is the bowl. Do I want it still
Chipped as it is and crazed,
Its lustrous cream no longer running
Over the body in fleet glaze,

I'm getting rid, getting shot, cleansing
Dark cupboards and fossil-deep
Drawers lined with historic newspaper.
I stop to read about the three-day-week.

Here are gewgaws with tarnished clasps
Here is the gravy-boat, the one item
Surviving from the wedding service.
Here's Ted Heath's improbable grin.

I flick the rim and it gives back a tang –
Yes, I remember that, the exact sound
Of early curiosity and boredom.
Bowl on my palm, I twist it round

And round again, unsure.
Do I hold or let it fall?

On looking through the handle of a cup

On looking through the handle of a cup
I spied a nest of green: the spout
Minus the can, a bunch of leaves
Big as my hand: two trees
In the palm of the wind,

On looking through the hole made by a pin
In a plane leaf twirled
All ways to catch the world
I saw a drop of rain, swollen
On the petal of a rose,

On looking through the fault in my eyes
With their arrhythmias of vision
I saw what no one has seen:
My cup-handle of a world,
My pinhole morning.

Ten Books

Jacketless, buckled, pressed from the voyage,
Ten books that once were crated to America
And back again,
That have known the salt sea's swing under them,
Oil stink, the deep throb of the engines
And quick hands putting them back on the shelves.

Spines torn, the paper wartime, the Faber
Font squarish and the dates in Roman:
The Waste Land and other poems,
Poems Newly Selected, Siegfried Sassoon –
How that name conjured with me
As a soldier kicked at a dead man.

MacNeice, freckled with brown
From many damps in many different houses.
On the inner page, under my father's autograph
An early flourish of blue crayon
Where I scribbled a figure so primitive
There are not even legs for it to walk upon.

Bowed, chipped, darkening, edge-worn
Sunned, loose, fading
Binding copy, reading copy, shaken:
Ten books that I have taken.
From the balcony on an August morning
I see the rest fly to the tip lorry

Where the sofa for a moment reposes
Legs in the air, grinning.
It is soaked through with music
But nothing will save it.
Behind it the sea makes the usual silveriness,
The café opens and the bikes whizz

From end to end of the promenade.
Meanwhile in my father's hand, a quotation
On the title page of Herbert Read's
Thirty-Five Poems: 'I absorbed Blake,
His strange beauty, his profound message,
His miraculous technique, and to emulate

Blake was to be my ambition
And my despair...' (Faber and Faber,
24 Russell Square.) I see my own hands
Smooth and small as they are not now
Lifting, turning, 'I am amazed
To find how much I owe to him.'

Subtraction

You always thought that you'd die mid-stride,
Sun on your left hand, darkness
Crossing you out in one swipe.

When you got on to subtraction
It was easy-peasy. Add one
At the top, take one from the next column.

Good at take-away, good at adding,
Revving up for the 11-plus
But no mathematician,

You stumbled upon infinity
With infinite terror, and knew
The limits of divinity –

What you'd been told was wrong.
If all you loved had been given
Then all could be taken.

You knew then that you must blot
In the blue notebook, trim
With happy pencil, the sum
Of what is when it is not.

My people

My people are the dying,
I am of their company
And they are mine,
We wake in the wan hour
Between three and four,
Listen to the rain
And consider our painkillers.
I lie here in the warm
With four pillows, a light
And the comfort of my phone
On which I sometimes compose,
And the words come easily
Bubbling like notes
From a bird that thinks it is dawn.

My people are the dying.
I reach out to them,
A company of suffering.
One falls by the roadside
And a boot stamps on him,
One lies in her cell, alone,
Without tenderness
Brutally handled
Towards her execution.
I can do nothing.
This is my vigil: the lit candle,
The pain, the breath of my people
Drawn in pain.

September Rain

Always rain, September rain,
The slipstream of the season,
Night of the equinox, the change.

There are three surfers out back.
Now the rain's pulse is doubled, the wave
Is not to be caught. Are they lost in the dark

Do they know where the coast is combed with light
Or is there only the swell, lifting
Back to the beginning

When they ran down the hill like children
Through this rain, September rain,
And the sea opened its breast to them?

I lie and listen
And the life in me stirs like a tide
That knows when it must be gone.

I am on the deep deep water
Lightly held by one ankle
Out of my depth, waiting.

Hold out your arms

Death, hold out your arms for me
Embrace me
Give me your motherly caress,
Through all this suffering
You have not forgotten me.

You are the bearded iris that bakes its rhizomes
Beside the wall,
Your scent flushes with loveliness,
Sherbet, pure iris
Lovely and intricate.

I am the child who stands by the wall
Not much taller than the iris.
The sun covers me
The day waits for me
In my funny dress.

Death, you heap into my arms
A basket of unripe damsons
Red crisscross straps that button behind me.
I don't know about school,
My knowledge is for papery bud covers
Tall stems and brown
Bees touching here and there, delicately
Before a swerve to the sun.

Death stoops over me
Her long skirts slide,
She knows I am shy.
Even the puffed sleeves on my white blouse
Embarrass me,
She will pick me up and hold me
So no one can see me,
I will scrub my hair into hers.

There, the iris increases
Note by note
As the wall gives back heat.
Death, there's no need to ask:
A mother will always lift a child
As a rhizome
Must lift up a flower
So you settle me
My arms twining,
Thighs gripping your hips
Where the swell of you is.

As you push back my hair
– Which could do with a comb
But never mind –
You murmur
'We're nearly there.'

(25 May 2017)